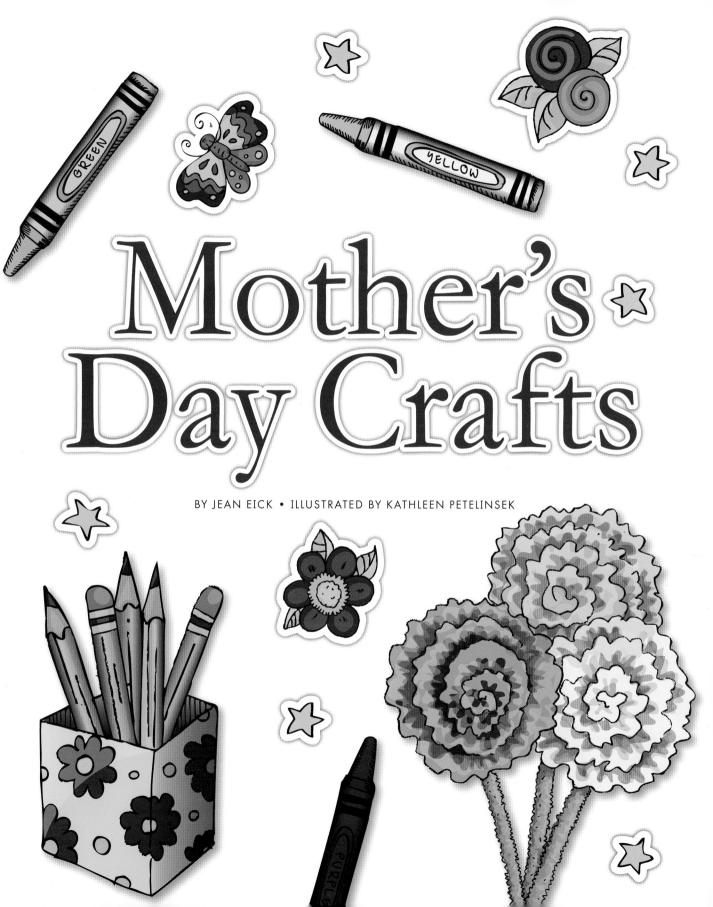

Mother's Day Crafts

BY JEAN EICK • ILLUSTRATED BY KATHLEEN PETELINSEK

Published by The Child's World®
1980 Lookout Drive
Mankato, MN 56003-1705
800-599-READ
www.childsworld.com

The Child's World®: Mary Berendes, Publishing Director
The Design Lab: Design and production

Library of Congress Cataloging-in-Publication Data
Eick, Jean, 1947–
  Mother's Day crafts / by Jean Eick; illustrated by Kathleen Petelinsek.
     p. cm.
  ISBN 978-1-60954-236-8 (library bound: alk. paper)
1. Holiday decorations—Juvenile literature. 2. Handicraft—Juvenile
literature. 3. Mother's Day—Juvenile literature. I. Petelinsek, Kathleen, ill.
II. Title.
  TT900.H6E332 2011
  745.594'1—dc22   2010035478

Printed in the United States of America
Mankato, MN
December, 2010
PA02071

Table of Contents

Happy Mother's Day!…4

Let's Begin!…6

C R A F T S

Pipe-cleaner Flowers…8

Tissue Flowers…10

Painted Pots…12

Pencil Holder…14

Flower Vase…16

Mother's Day Cards…18

Envelopes…20

Activities…22

Glossary…23

Find More Crafts…23

Index…24

Happy Mother's Day!

Mother's Day is a very special **holiday**. It's a time to show how much people care about their mothers. It's also a time to say "Thank you." On Mother's Day, many people give their moms homemade gifts and decorations.

Mother's Day is **celebrated** all over the world. It happens on different days in different countries. In the United States, Mother's Day is always on the second Sunday in May. It's a time to remember all of the mothers in the world and to thank them for all that they do. Some families treat their moms to a meal at a restaurant. Other people give their moms gifts or cards. Wherever you are in the world, Mother's Day is a time to celebrate how much we love our mothers!

Let's Begin!

1 This book is full of great ideas you can make to celebrate Mother's Day. There are ideas for decorations, gifts, and cards. There are activities at the end of this book, too!

2 Before you start making any craft, be sure to read the **directions**. Make sure you look at the pictures too—they will help you understand what to do. Go through the list of things you'll need and get everything together. When you're ready, find a good place to work. Now you can begin making your crafts!

Pipe-cleaner Flowers

Moms love flowers. Instead of giving her real ones,
try making some of these for her instead.

THINGS YOU'LL NEED

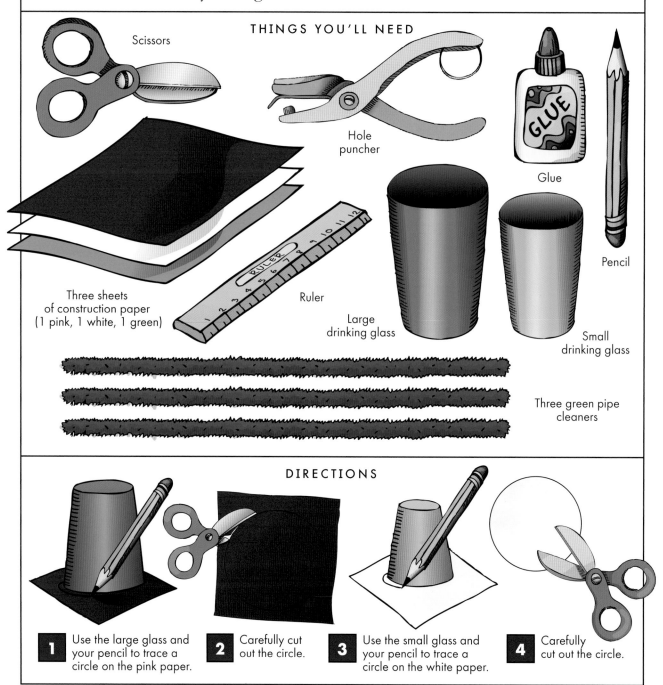

Scissors

Hole puncher

Glue

Pencil

Three sheets
of construction paper
(1 pink, 1 white, 1 green)

Ruler

Large
drinking glass

Small
drinking glass

Three green pipe
cleaners

DIRECTIONS

1 Use the large glass and your pencil to trace a circle on the pink paper.

2 Carefully cut out the circle.

3 Use the small glass and your pencil to trace a circle on the white paper.

4 Carefully cut out the circle.

5 Glue the middle of the two circles together.

6 Make small cuts in both circles.

7 Use the hole puncher to make a hole in the middle of the circles.

8 Use your pencil to draw two leaves on the green paper. Use your ruler to be sure each leaf is 4 inches long and 3/4 inches wide.

9 Carefully cut out the leaves.

10 Punch a hole in each leaf that is 1/2 inches from the flat end.

11 Pull the green pipe cleaners through the holes (one through the flower and one through each leaf). Pinch the ends of the pipe cleaners into a circle so they don't fall back through the holes.

12 Fold and glue the flat end of each leaf together. Be sure to hold each leaf until the glue dries!

13 Twist the leaf pipe cleaners around the flower pipe cleaner.

Tissue Flowers

Here are even more flowers you can give your mom.

THINGS YOU'LL NEED

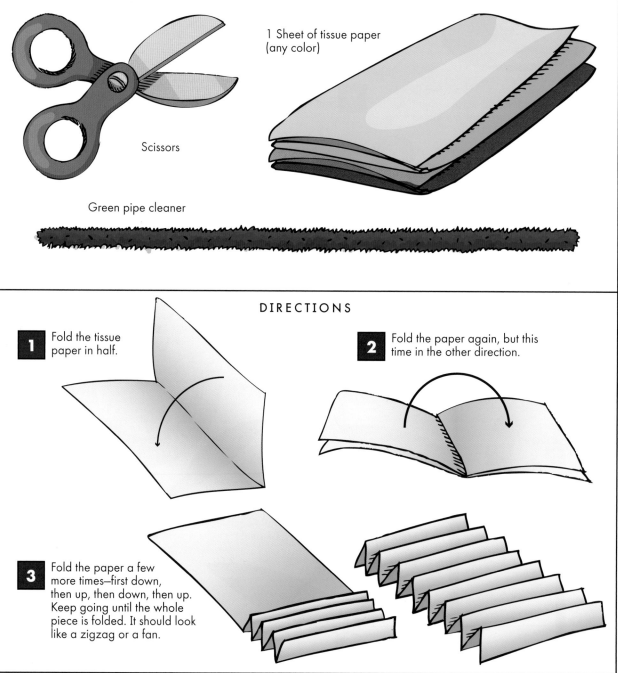

Scissors

1 Sheet of tissue paper
(any color)

Green pipe cleaner

DIRECTIONS

1 Fold the tissue
paper in half.

2 Fold the paper again, but this
time in the other direction.

3 Fold the paper a few
more times—first down,
then up, then down, then up.
Keep going until the whole
piece is folded. It should look
like a zigzag or a fan.

4 Wrap the green pipe cleaner around the middle of the paper.

5 Carefully cut the ends of the paper. Try cutting in wavy lines or zigzags.

6 Slowly open up the paper. You'll see the flower appear! Now make more flowers just like this one, but in different colors! You can even use two pieces of paper (in different colors) to make an extra-colorful flower.

Painted Pots

Your mom can use these pretty pots for planting or to put candles inside.

THINGS YOU'LL NEED

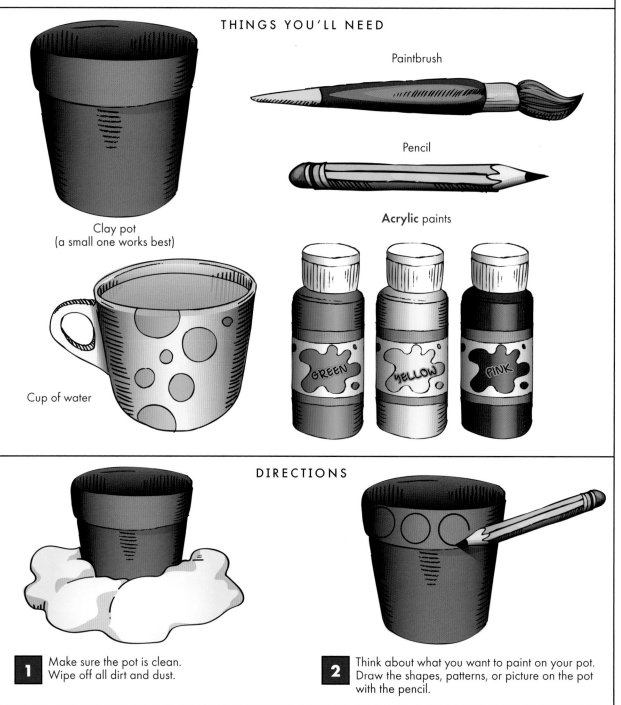

Clay pot
(a small one works best)

Cup of water

Paintbrush

Pencil

Acrylic paints

GREEN   YELLOW   PINK

DIRECTIONS

1 Make sure the pot is clean. Wipe off all dirt and dust.

2 Think about what you want to paint on your pot. Draw the shapes, patterns, or picture on the pot with the pencil.

3 Use the paintbrush and paints to paint along the lines you've just drawn.

4 Clean your brush using the cup of water if you want to use another color.

5 If you want to use one color on top of another, be sure the bottom color is dry before you start.

6 When you are finished painting, let the pot dry all the way. Now it's ready to be given as a beautiful Mother's Day gift!

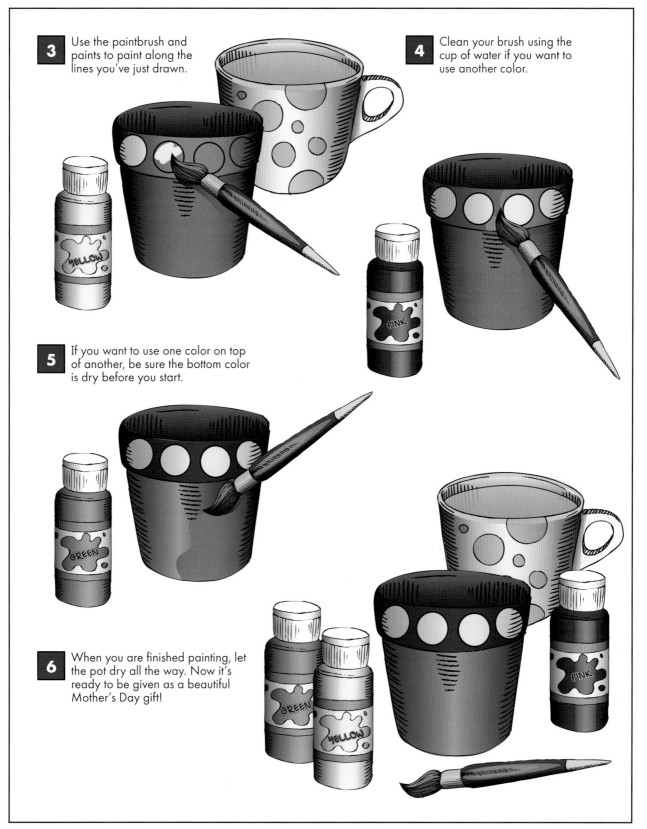

Pencil Holder

This looks great almost anywhere—especially on Mom's desk or in her kitchen!

THINGS YOU'LL NEED

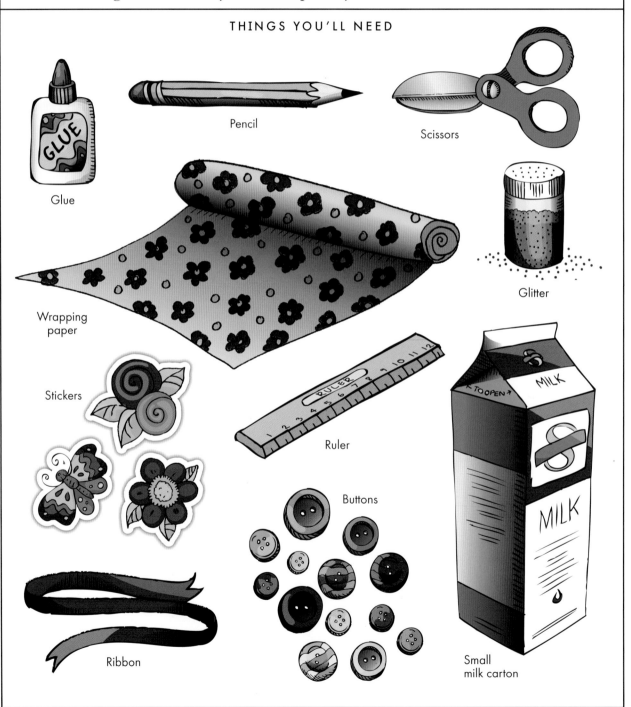

Glue

Pencil

Scissors

Wrapping paper

Glitter

Stickers

Ruler

Buttons

MILK

MILK

Ribbon

Small milk carton

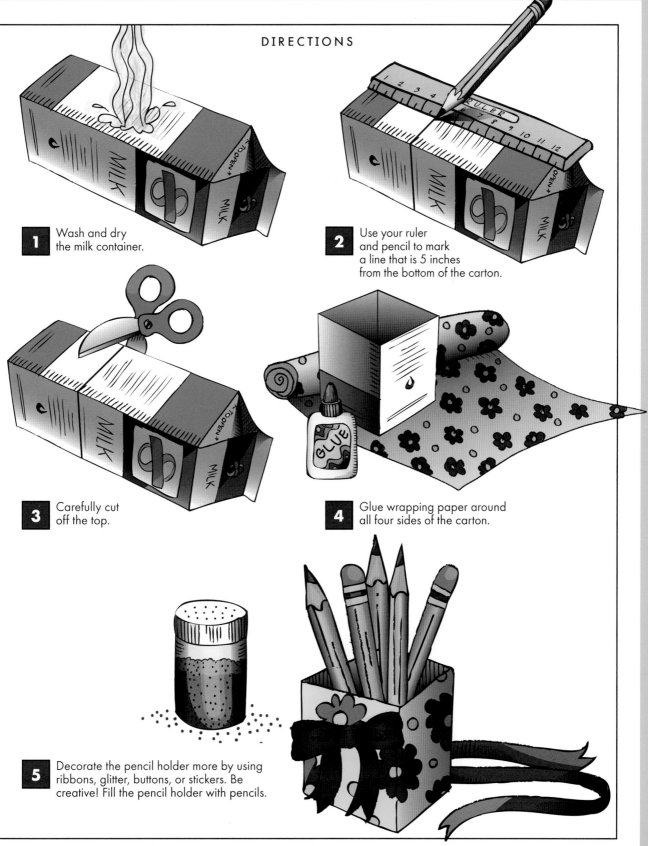

DIRECTIONS

1 Wash and dry the milk container.

2 Use your ruler and pencil to mark a line that is 5 inches from the bottom of the carton.

3 Carefully cut off the top.

4 Glue wrapping paper around all four sides of the carton.

5 Decorate the pencil holder more by using ribbons, glitter, buttons, or stickers. Be creative! Fill the pencil holder with pencils.

15

Flower Vase

This vase is an easy gift you can make for your mom.
Fill it with the flowers you made on pages 8–11.

THINGS YOU'LL NEED

Scissors

Stickers

Wrapping
paper

Buttons

Tape or
glue

GLUE

A salad-
dressing bottle

Ribbon

Glitter

DIRECTIONS

1 Wash and dry the salad-dressing bottle. Cut small pieces of wrapping paper. Squares or strips work best. Tape or glue the wrapping paper all over the bottle.

2 Decorate the bottle more by using ribbons, glitter, buttons, or stickers. Be creative!

3 You can add some of the flowers you created on pages 8–11.

Mother's Day Cards

Mother's Day is a great time to give your mom a special card.
Write a nice message inside thanking her for all her hard work!

THINGS YOU'LL NEED

Scissors

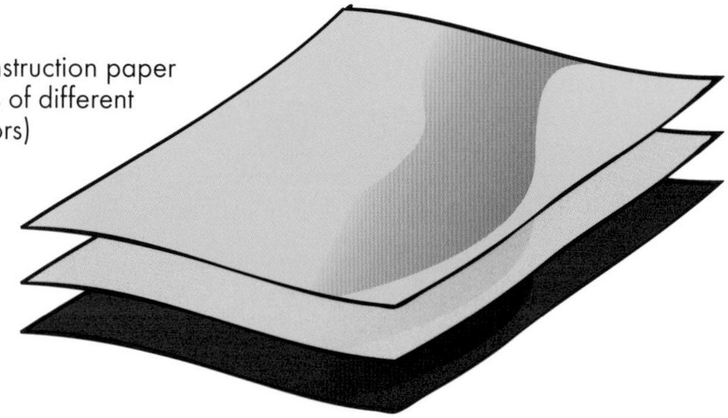

Construction paper
(lots of different
colors)

Glitter

Buttons

Glue

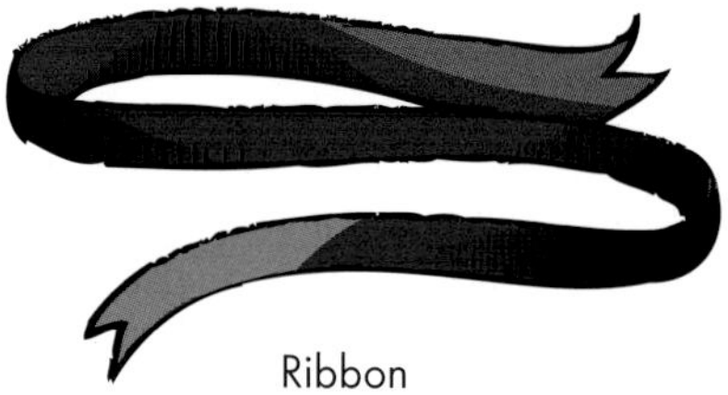

Ribbon

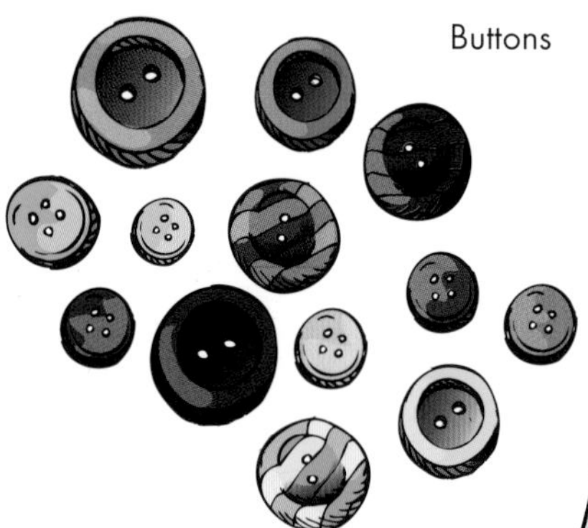

Crayons, markers, or paint

Stickers or
magazine pictures

Pencil

DIRECTIONS FOR CARD ONE

1 Fold a piece of construction paper to the size you want it to be. Folding once will make a large card. Folding it twice will make a smaller card.

2 Decorate the front of the card any way you'd like. You can use ribbons, buttons, glitter, and stickers—be creative! Write a message on the inside of the card. You can decorate the inside, too. Don't forget to sign your name!

DIRECTIONS FOR OTHER CARDS

1 You can make Mother's Day cards in many different ways. Here are some ideas for making your cards even more special! Place your hand on the front of the card and use your pencil to trace around it. Then decorate your handprint with crayons, markers, or glitter.

2 For a flower card, glue colored strips and a cotton ball to the front of the card. They should make a flower shape.

3 For a picture card, find a nice photograph of you and your mom together. Glue the picture to the front of the card and decorate all around it.

Envelopes

You can make your own envelopes to fit your homemade cards.

THINGS YOU'LL NEED

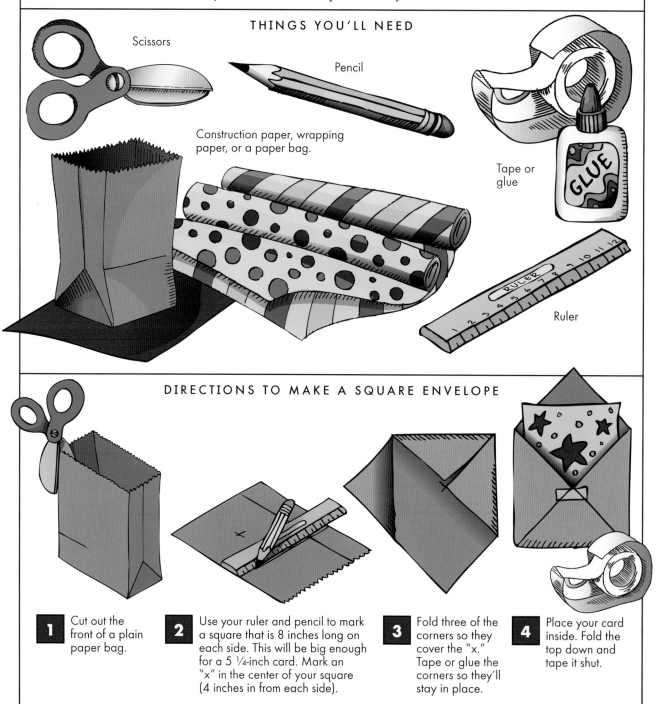

Scissors

Pencil

Construction paper, wrapping paper, or a paper bag.

Tape or glue

GLUE

RULER

Ruler

DIRECTIONS TO MAKE A SQUARE ENVELOPE

1 Cut out the front of a plain paper bag.

2 Use your ruler and pencil to mark a square that is 8 inches long on each side. This will be big enough for a 5 ¼-inch card. Mark an "x" in the center of your square (4 inches in from each side).

3 Fold three of the corners so they cover the "x." Tape or glue the corners so they'll stay in place.

4 Place your card inside. Fold the top down and tape it shut.

DIRECTIONS TO MAKE AN ENVELOPE THAT'S NOT SQUARE

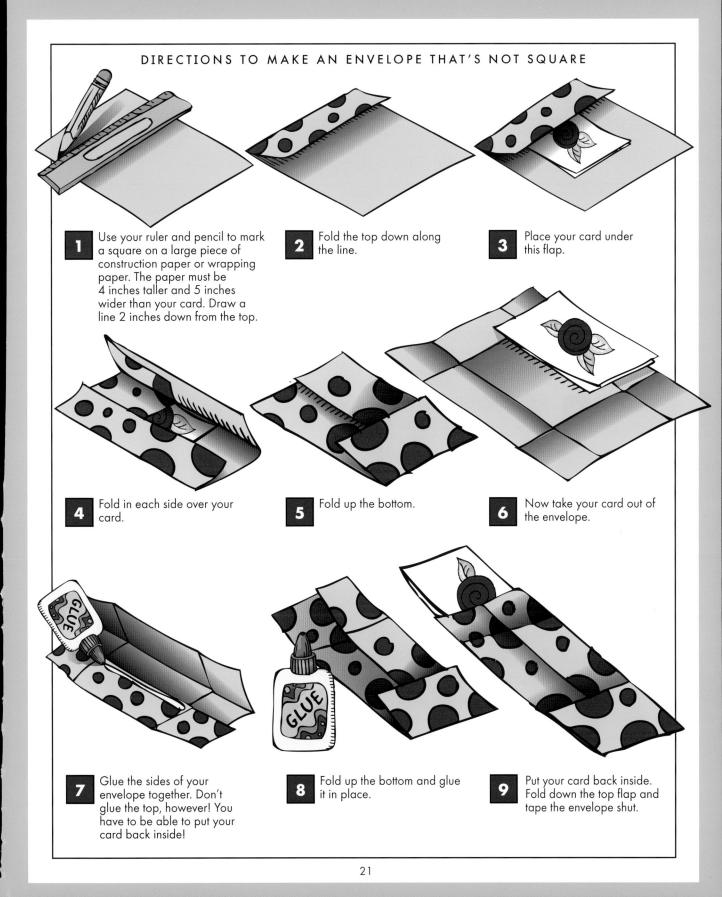

1 Use your ruler and pencil to mark a square on a large piece of construction paper or wrapping paper. The paper must be 4 inches taller and 5 inches wider than your card. Draw a line 2 inches down from the top.

2 Fold the top down along the line.

3 Place your card under this flap.

4 Fold in each side over your card.

5 Fold up the bottom.

6 Now take your card out of the envelope.

7 Glue the sides of your envelope together. Don't glue the top, however! You have to be able to put your card back inside!

8 Fold up the bottom and glue it in place.

9 Put your card back inside. Fold down the top flap and tape the envelope shut.

Activities

Here are some fun things to do to celebrate Mother's Day.
Try them all and show your mom how special she is!

1 Write notes to your mom thanking her for the things she does. Here are some ideas:

"Thanks, Mom, for reading to me!"

"Thanks, Mom, for washing my clothes!"

"Thanks, Mom, for baking my favorite cookies!"

2 Set the table before anyone else does. Tie ribbons around all the napkins. Use decorations from this book to decorate the table. Don't forget your paper flowers!

3 Tie a pretty ribbon around your mom's favorite candy bar. Put it on her pillow for a bedtime surprise. Be sure to leave it next to a card you've made for her!

4 Start a **flowerbed** with your mom. Plant some flower seeds inside a pot or container. Water the seeds and give them plenty of sunlight. When the seeds have sprouted, bring the pot outside and help your mom plant them in her flowerbed.

Glossary

acrylic (uh-KRIL-ik) Acrylic paints are thick and dry quickly. They are good to use in art projects.

celebrated (SEL-uh-bray-ted) When people celebrate something, they do something happy and fun. Mother's Day is celebrated all over the world.

directions (dir-EK-shunz) Directions are the steps for how to do something. You should follow the directions in this book to make your crafts.

holiday (HOL-uh-day) A holiday is a time for celebration, such as Christmas or Valentine's Day. Mother's Day is a holiday.

flowerbed (FLAUW-er-bed) A flowerbed is an area where flowers and plants are grown.

Find More Crafts

BOOKS

Ross, Kathy, and Sharon Lane Holm (illustrator). *All New Crafts for Mother's and Father's Day*. Minneapolis, MN: Millbrook Press, 2007.

West, Robin, Robert L Wolfe, Diane Wolfe, and Jackie Urbanovic (illustrator). *My Very Own Mother's Day: A Book of Cooking and Crafts*. Minneapolis, MN: Carolrhoda Books, Inc., 1996.

WEB SITES

Visit our Web site for links to more crafts: childsworld.com/links

Note to Parents, Teachers, and Librarians: We routinely verify our Web links to make sure they are safe and active sites. So encourage your readers to check them out!

Index

activities, 22

cards, 18

celebrating, 5

date, 5

envelopes, 20

flower vase, 16

flowerbed, 22

history, 5

painted pots, 12

pencil holder, 14

pipe-cleaner flowers, 8

tissue flowers, 10

ABOUT THE AUTHOR

Jean Eick has written over 200 books for children over the past forty years. She has written biographies, craft books, and many titles on nature and science. Jean lives in Lake Tahoe with her husband and enjoys hiking in the mountains, reading, and doing volunteer work.